D1356020

CHRISTIANITY
AND THE
CRISIS OF CULTURES

JOSEPH CARDINAL RATZINGER
(Pope Benedict XVI)

CHRISTIANITY AND THE CRISIS OF CULTURES

Introduction by Marcello Pera

Translated by Brian McNeil

IGNATIUS PRESS   SAN FRANCISCO

Title of Italian original:
L'Europa di Benedetto nella crisi delle culture
© 2005 by Edizioni Cantagalli, Siena

Cover photograph:
Saint Patrick's Cathedral, New York
© Kevin Forest / Photodisc

Cover design by Roxanne Mei Lum

© 2006 Libreria Editrice Vaticana
© 2006 by Ignatius Press, San Francisco
All rights reserved
ISBN 978-1-58617-142-1
ISBN 1-58617-142-9
Library of Congress Control Number 2005909729
Printed in the United States of America ∞

CONTENTS

INTRODUCTION

A Proposal That Should Be Accepted

by
Marcello Pera

At the origins of what Joseph Ratzinger (now Pope Benedict XVI) calls in this book "the most radical contradiction" that has developed in Europe lies the "great division" brought about by the scientific revolution.

Galileo, in his endeavor to avoid a conflict with the Church over the relationship between the new Copernican astronomy and the interpretation of Scripture in keeping with Aristotelianism, put forward two theses.

The first thesis maintains that if Scripture is correctly interpreted, it is necessarily in agreement with astronomy, because, as Galileo wrote in his letter of December 21, 1613, to Don Benedetto Castelli:

> Sacred Scripture and nature proceed equally from the Divine Word, the one dictated by the Holy Spirit, the other a most observant executor of the orders of God. When Scripture accommodates

itself to our understanding of the universe, it says many things that diverge from the absolute truth, on points of detail and in terms of the meaning of words. . . . It seems that what our eyes observe of the workings of nature or what our senses experience or the conclusions we necessarily draw from the demonstrations of science should not at all be called into question by passages of Scripture that appear to say something different. For not every single word of Scripture is binding on us with exactly the same force as every working of nature.

The second thesis is that Scripture and astronomy are dealing with different things, the former with the salvation of men, the latter with factual questions. As Galileo wrote to Madame Cristina di Lorena in 1615:

And if the same Holy Spirit has intentionally refrained from teaching us propositions of this kind [that is, of astronomy], since these have nothing to do with his own true intention— which is our salvation—how can one then assert that it is absolutely necessary to hold *this* position rather than *that,* so that one is *de fide,* the other erroneous? . . . Here, I would repeat something I once heard from an ecclesiastical personage of the most eminent rank, namely, that it is the intention of the Holy Spirit to teach us how to go to heaven, not how heaven goes.

We can call the first point *the thesis of convergence* or of *unity* between science and Scripture and the second *the thesis of separation* or of *diversity* between the sphere of scientific research and the sphere of religious salvation.

At least *prima facie*, the two theses are not incompatible, and in the case of Galileo, a great scientist and a deeply convinced believer, they were certainly not so. Both theses maintain the possibility of reconciling science and religion, although they do so in different ways. For the thesis of convergence, there cannot be conflicts between truths of science and truths of the faith, because both "Sacred Scripture and nature proceed equally from the divine Word" and advance *in harmony*, so that every scientific progress becomes a hermeneutical progress. In the same way, for the thesis of separation, there cannot be conflicts, because both advance *independently*, each in its own autonomous and separate sphere and with different methods, criteria, and sources.

But although these theses may appear incompatible, in reality they are saying something different about the theoretical perspectives and about the practical consequences. And both theses have left a profound mark on European culture.

From the theoretical point of view, the thesis of convergence sees the discourse of science and the discourse of faith as two authentic *forms of knowledge* that are (or ought to be) in harmony. However, the thesis of separation sees scientific knowledge as authentic knowledge, because the discourse of faith is not knowledge, properly speaking, but *something one believes*. In the first case, knowledge is *one*: man knows (in the full sense of this word) *both* his world *and* the meaning of his world. In the second case, knowledge is—or ends up as—*fragmented*: there exist a public and objective scientific knowledge and a private and subjective religious belief.

What are the practical consequences? For the thesis of convergence, the science that deals with the world ought to feel itself bound to the religion of Scripture, so that it can attain harmony with the latter. For the thesis of separation, science is free and must proceed autonomously, even if Scripture should oppose it on one point or another. Science "knows", and technology "can". But if science is free to know, then technology is free to be able to do anything. Religion cannot pose any obstacle here, since it operates on a different level.

This is the "great division" that Galileo set in motion. It was the first such division, and others soon followed: between truths of faith and truths of science; truths of morality and truths of legal rights; divine truths and truths of the state; public truths and private truths. Everywhere—from science to society to the individual life—European and Western man has produced and experienced a schism, a separation between that which *is* and as such can be verified scientifically (with "what our senses experience" and "the demonstrations of science") and that which *ought to be* and which is based on sources that are not scientific or rational (customs, beliefs, the faith).

This identification of the rational with the scientific and this gulf that yawns between science, morality, and religion are the basic characteristic of modernity. "Hume's law" (that is, that it is a logical error to infer an "ought" from an "is") is an axiom of our way of thinking. This is the "great division" and the cultural and political banner of what is rather imprecisely known as the "Enlightenment".

What can I know? What ought I to do? What am I permitted to hope? If the unity of knowledge is shattered, there is no longer any relationship between these three questions. Each is left to its own devices, without any hope of receiving a reply that would be valid for the other questions, too. Kant, who asked himself these questions more systematically than anyone else and who saw more clearly than anyone else the danger of separating them, hurried to repair the breaches. In his endeavor to provide a proper foundation for science without destroying morality and faith, he made the existence of God, of liberty, and of the immortality of the soul "postulates of the practical reason", without which it is not possible to act in a moral manner or to attain the highest good. Following this line of argument, morality and religion must accept that which science excludes (because it cannot be contained within the limits of the reason). Science does not prove the existence of good or evil, and it demonstrates neither the existence nor the non-existence of God; but morality and religion have need of God. Scientific knowledge prescinds from God, but moral action requires him. Here we have a genuine schism. The solution thought out by Kant did not succeed in overcoming it, because once it had taken hold, the logic of separation was more powerful than the logic of unification.

The rationality of the Enlightenment bore prodigious and precious fruit. Without this, the great scientific, technological, economic, civil, and constitutional advances that have irrevocably changed the face of Europe and of all the West are inexplicable. The chain is long, but there is no break in it: after the scientific revolution came the technological revolution, the industrial revolution, and then the revolutions in politics, in the life of society, and in the rights of the individual.

Are these advances universal? *Yes*, at least to a large extent, because they represent important, fundamental, and precious gains. Their inherent vigor won them acceptance; they are capable of further development; and they remain very attractive.

And are these advances also sufficient in themselves? *No*, because ultimately, as Benedict XVI says in this book, they carry a price that we are paying today above all: marginalization, the triumph of subjectivity, and the imprisonment of the divine, of the sacred, of God in a ghetto. In European culture, the price we pay is the banishment of Christianity, not only from the life of states, but also from the life of civic society. In the European Constitution, the price is the refusal even to recall that our continent was the Christian continent. In the life of Europe, the price is the confusion of people's consciences. As the Pope writes here, "Europe has developed a culture that, in a manner hitherto unknown to humanity, excludes God from public awareness."

It is true, as he also notes, that "the Enlightenment has a Christian origin": Galileo is the best testimony to this fact. Today, however, this origin is vanishing from people's memories, and the rationality of the Enlightenment is becoming arid. In this process of drying up, science produces an exclusive belief in its own potential, the autonomy of the non-religious sphere generates laicism, and that very "secularization" which for centuries was a gain for individuals, peoples, and states turns against itself. Individuals experience alienation, peoples lose their identity, and states are in thrall to weakness, uncertainty, inertia, and fear.

One last effect of the rationality of the Enlightenment—or more precisely, of the feeble imitators of Galileo and Kant who have promoted a rationality that trusts exclusively in science and is hostile to the Church—can be seen in today's discussions of bioethical questions. In this field, the "great division" produced by the scientific revolution shows how optimistic was the thesis of the separation of the different spheres of competence and how precarious is the balance between science and technology, on the one hand, and morality and religion, on the other.

The rationality of the Enlightenment has bequeathed us a principle we all consider sacred and inviolable. To quote the Pope, this is "one single value [that seems] not to be the object of discussion, since it is indisputable, and [that] has therefore become a filter through which every other 'value' is passed, namely, the right of the individual to express himself freely, without any impositions from outside himself, at least so long as his freedom does not infringe the rights of others." This right, too, which is (or is derived from) the person's right to respect, has a Christian origin: we read in Genesis that "man was made in the image of God", and "God said, 'Let us make man in our own image and likeness.'"

When the Enlightenment transformed these words of God into a human right, this was a great advance. But when other advances joined this one—scientific freedom, the autonomy of technology, women's self-determination—this resulted in problems that are difficult to solve.

Among the most difficult of these problems that face us today are the questions of bioethics, in particular that of justifying why—under the terms of legislation concerning abortion and artificial fertility—the right of the fetus or embryo not to be hurt or killed must yield to the right to individual freedom. The reason for this is not clear. Is it perhaps because the fetus and embryo are not persons? Perhaps because they are "small", and the life of little ones can be sacrificed in favor of that of adults? Perhaps because a "little murder" is not a genuine murder? Or perhaps because the embryo and the fetus are not included among those "others" who represent the absolute limit of "our" right to individual liberty?

This is where we see the limitation of the "great division". It is not true to say that the separation of spheres—scientific, legal, moral, religious—always guarantees equilibrium and never leads to conflicts between the various spheres. The opposite is true! Often, free action in one sphere interacts negatively with free action in another. If God is expelled from the scientific sphere, religion is expelled from the life of man. If morality is expelled from law, our laws are deprived of all values. If science and technology enjoy an unlimited guarantee, progress can become blind and destructive.

It is impossible to resolve these problems by endeavoring to return to the old pre-Galilean alliance of one single form of knowledge that would embrace everything harmoniously. Here, too, original sin has its effects: once one has eaten from the tree of knowledge, paradise is lost. Nevertheless, it remains possible and necessary to recall the limits of science and to set boundaries to what the law can do. We are paying the price of the gap between the speed with which science and technology offer us instruments to satisfy our desires and the slowness with which we succeed in understanding these instruments and mastering them; between wisdom and knowledge; between the rationality of the Enlightenment and our salvation.

How can we overcome this gap? And how can we face the challenges this gap produces? In the first essay in this book, the Pope makes a *proposal to those outside the Church*:

> In the age of the Enlightenment, the attempt was made to understand and define the essential norms of morality by saying that these would be valid *etsi Deus non daretur*, even if God did not exist. . . . We must . . . reverse the axiom of the Enlightenment and say: Even the one who does not succeed in finding the path to accepting the existence of God ought nevertheless to try to live and to direct his life *veluti si Deus daretur*, as if God did indeed exist.

This proposal should be accepted, this challenge welcomed, for one basic reason: because the one outside the Church who acts *veluti si Deus daretur* becomes *more responsible in moral terms*. He will no longer say that an embryo is a "thing" or a "lump of cells" or "genetic material". He will no longer say that the elimination of an embryo or a fetus does not infringe any rights. He will no longer say that a desire that can be satisfied by some technical means is automatically a right that should be claimed and granted. He will no longer say that all scientific and technological progress is per se a liberation or a moral advance. He will no longer say that the only rationality and the only form of life outside the Church are scientific rationality and an existence bereft of values. He will no longer act as only half a man, one lacerated and divided. He will no longer think that a democracy consisting of the mere counting of numbers is an adequate substitute for wisdom.

When a believer suggests that he should act *veluti si Deus daretur*, the non-believer in the secular sphere can and should respond affirmatively. But precisely because he is not a believer, he has the right and the duty in all honesty to make some things clear. Even the non-believer outside the Church must think of God as if he existed—but for him, this is not the God of the Church. It is a God who does not have a defined face, who does not have dogmas that cannot be "improved", who does not have revelations that cannot be "revised", who does not have interpreters against whose word no appeal is possible, who does not have specific professions of faith, who does not have exclusive rites. This God is the God of his conscience, the God who makes him aware of his finitude and his wretchedness but also of his greatness, the God who makes him a moral agent, the God who mysteriously punishes him and approves of him, the God of his anguish and of his exultation.

Between this God outside the Church and the Christian God stands revelation, the historical event that manifested itself at one point in the past, and the perception of a Person who continues to manifest himself. For the Christian, this event and this Person are the essence of his faith, which, as the Pope writes, "is the fundamental act of Christian existence". For the one outside the Church, this same event and this same Person are a part of his culture, of his history, of his identity.

But in terms of the effects on individual and societal life, there are *no* differences between the God outside the Church and the Christian God. At least here, on the Christian continent—and wherever the Christian continent has conquered other hearts and minds—we act *veluti si Deus daretur.* We act in liberty and equality as if we were all sons of God; we respect each other as if we were made in the image of God; we love one another as if we were responding thereby to an order given by God; we despair over one another as if we had been abandoned by God; we console one another as if we hoped in God; we reward one another as if we were giving thanks to God; we punish one another as if we were obliged one day to render an account to God. Accordingly, each one of us lives as if he were a man of God.

If, as the Holy Father writes, "the splendor of the fact that he is the image of God . . . no longer shines upon this man" today—since ours is an age of agnosticism, of relativism, of disenchantment, of presumption—this is one more reason to accept the proposal he makes to those outside the Church. We would all benefit by this, not only at the point where we stand today, but also in view of the heights to which we could in fact rise, each individual and all of us together: ourselves, our peoples, our laws, our Europe, and this civilization of ours that Augustine, Thomas, Machiavelli, Galileo, Newton, Kant, Einstein, and so many others have forged with their genius—and at the same time, a civilization that comes down to us from Golgotha and from Sinai.

Veluti si Deus daretur. This is a wager: the stake we invest is our own commitment, and the winnings are our salvation.

THE CRISIS OF CULTURES

I

Reflections on Cultures That Are in Conflict Today

We are living in a period of great dangers and of great opportunities both for man and for the world, a period that also imposes a great responsibility on us all. During the past century, the possibilities available to man for dominion over matter have grown in a manner we may truly call unimaginable. But the fact that he has power over the world has also meant that man's destructive power has reached dimensions that can sometimes make us shudder. Here, one thinks spontaneously of the threat of terrorism, this new war without national borders and without lines of battle. The fear that terrorists may get hold of nuclear and biological weapons is not unfounded, and this has induced even states under the rule of law to have recourse to internal systems of security similar to those that once existed only in dictatorships; and yet, the feeling remains that all these precautions will never really be enough, since a completely global control is neither possible nor desirable. Less visible, but not for that reason less disturbing, are the possibilities of self-manipulation that man has acquired. He has investigated the farthest recesses of his being, he has deciphered the components of the human being, and now he is able, so to speak, to "construct" man on his own. This means that man enters the world, no longer as a gift of the Creator, but as the product of our activity—and a product that can be selected according to requirements that we ourselves stipulate. In this way, the splendor of the fact that he is the image of God—the source of his dignity and of his inviolability—no longer shines upon this man; his only splendor is the power of human capabilities. Man is nothing more now than the image of man—but of what man? To this we must add the great problems of our planet: the inequality in the distribution of the goods of the earth, increasing poverty, the depletion and exploitation of the earth and of its resources, famine, the illnesses that threaten all the world, the clash of cultures. All this demonstrates that the growth of our possibilities is not matched by an equal development of our moral energy. Moral strength has not grown in tandem with the development of science; on the contrary, it has diminished, because the technological mentality confines morality to the subjective sphere. Our need, however, is for a public morality, a morality capable of responding to the threats that impose such a burden on the existence of us all. The true and gravest danger of the present moment is precisely this imbalance between technological possibilities and moral energy. The security we all need as a presupposition of our freedom and dignity cannot ultimately be derived from technical systems of control. It can come only from the moral strength of man, and where this is lacking or insufficient, the power man has will be transformed more and more into a power of destruction.

It is indeed true that a new moralism exists today. Its key words are justice, peace, and the conservation of creation, and these are words that recall essential moral values, of which we genuinely stand in need. But this moralism remains vague and almost inevitably remains confined to the sphere of party politics, where it is primarily a claim addressed to others, rather than a personal duty in our own daily life. For what does "justice" mean? Who defines it? What promotes peace? In the last decades, we have seen plenty of evidence on the streets and squares of our cities of how pacifism can be perverted into a destructive anarchism or, indeed, into terrorism. The political moralism of the 1970s, the roots of which are far from dead, was a moralism that succeeded in fascinating even young people who were full of ideals. But it was a moralism that took the wrong direction, since it lacked the serenity born of rationality. In the last analysis, it attached a higher value to the political utopia than to the dignity of the individual, and it showed itself capable of despising man in the name of great objectives. The political moralism we have experienced, and still witness today, is far from opening the path to a real regeneration: instead, it blocks the way. Consequently, the same is true of a Christianity and a theology that reduce the core of the message of Jesus, that is, the "kingdom of God", to the "values of the kingdom", identifying these values with the great slogans of political moralism while at the same time proclaiming that these slogans are the synthesis of the religions. In this way, they forget God, although it is precisely he who is both the subject and the cause of the kingdom. All that remains in the place of God are the big words (and values) that are open to any kind of abuse.

This brief look at the situation of the world leads us to reflect on the situation of Christianity today and, hence, on the foundations on which Europe rests. We can say that while Europe once was the Christian continent, it was also the birthplace of that new scientific rationality which has given us both enormous possibilities and enormous menaces. Naturally, Christianity did not begin in Europe, and this means that it cannot be classified as a European religion or as the religion of the European cultural sphere. But it was precisely in Europe that Christianity took on its most efficacious cultural and intellectual form, and this is why it remains intimately linked in a very special way to Europe. On the other hand, it is also true that this Europe, from the Renaissance onward and in a fully fledged manner since the age of the Enlightenment, has developed precisely that scientific rationality which led to the geographical unity of the world and to the encounter between the continents and cultures in the age of the great discoveries. This same rationality leaves its imprint on all the world today in a much deeper way, thanks to the technological culture that science has made possible. Indeed, in a certain sense, scientific rationality is imposing uniformity on the world. In the wake of this form of rationality, Europe has developed a culture that, in a manner hitherto unknown to mankind, excludes God from public awareness. His existence may be denied altogether or considered unprovable and uncertain and, hence, as something belonging to the sphere of subjective choices. In either case, God is irrelevant to public life. This is a purely functional rationality that has shaken the moral consciousness in a way completely unknown to the cultures that existed previously, since it maintains that only that which can be demonstrated experimentally is "rational". Since morality belongs to a different sphere altogether, it disappears as a specific category; but since we do after all need some kind of morality, it has to be discovered anew in some other way. In a world based on calculations, it is the calculation of consequences that determines what should be considered moral and immoral. In this way, the category of the good vanishes, as Kant clearly showed. Nothing is good or evil in itself; everything depends on the consequences that may be thought to ensue upon an action. If, then, it is true to say that Christianity has found its most efficacious form in Europe, it is also true to say that a culture has developed in Europe that is the most radical contradiction not only of Christianity, but of all the religious and moral traditions of humanity. This shows us that Europe is going through a genuine "traction" (to use a medical term), and we can understand how deep-rooted are the tensions that our continent must face up to. Above all, it is here that we also see the responsibility we Europeans must shoulder in this moment of history: in the debate about the definition of Europe and its new political shape, we are not fighting some nostalgic battle in the "rearguard" of history. Rather,

we are taking seriously our tremendous responsibility for humanity today.

Let us look more closely at this antagonism
between the two cultures that have both left
their mark on Europe. In the debate about the
preamble to the European Constitution, this antagonism has come to light in two controversies:
the question of the reference to God in the
Constitution and the question of mentioning
the Christian roots of Europe. We are told that
we need not be alarmed, since article 52 of the
Constitution guarantees the institutional rights
of the churches. But this in fact means that in
the life of Europe, the churches are assigned
their place on the level of day-to-day political
compromises; but the message they proclaim is
not allowed to make any impact on the level of
the foundations on which Europe rests. Only
superficial reasons are given in the public debate
for this clear refusal, and it is clear that such
justifications conceal the true motivation instead
of disclosing it. The claim that a mention of the
Christian roots of Europe would wound the
feelings of the many non-Christians who live in
this continent is not particularly convincing,

since this basically involves a historical fact that no one can seriously deny. Naturally, this historical observation also contains a reference to the present, since the mention of the roots indicates the remaining sources of moral orientation, which is one factor in the identity of the formation known as "Europe". Who would be offended by this? Whose identity is threatened thereby? The Muslims, who so often tend to be mentioned in this context, feel threatened, not by the foundations of our Christian morality, but by the cynicism of a secularized culture that denies its own foundations. Nor are our Jewish fellow citizens offended by the reference to the Christian roots of Europe, since these roots go back to Mount Sinai and bear the imprint of the voice that rang out on the mountain of God. We are united with the Jews in those great basic orientations given to man by the Ten Commandments. The same applies to the reference to God: it is not the mention of God that offends those who belong to other religions; rather, it is the attempt to construct the human community in a manner that absolutely excludes God.

The motivations of this double refusal are

deeper than one might suspect from the reasons we actually hear. They presuppose the idea that only the radical culture born of the Enlightenment, which has attained its full development in our own age, can be constitutive of European identity. Alongside this culture, various religious cultures with their respective rights can coexist, on condition (and to the degree) that they respect the criteria of the Enlightenment culture and subordinate themselves to it. This Enlightenment culture is substantially defined by the rights to liberty. Its starting point is that liberty is a fundamental value and the criterion of everything else: the freedom of choice in matters of religion, which includes the religious neutrality of the state; the liberty to express one's own opinion, on condition that it does not call precisely this canon into question; the democratic ordering of the state, that is, the parliamentary control of the organs of state; the freedom to form political parties; the independence of those who administer the law; and finally, the protection of the rights of man and the prohibition of discrimination. On this point, the canon is still in the process of formation, since there exist

34

contrasting human rights, as we see in the conflict between a woman's right to freedom and the unborn child's right to life. The concept of discrimination is constantly enlarged, and this means that the prohibition of discrimination can be transformed more and more into a limitation on the freedom of opinion and on religious liberty. Very soon, it will no longer be possible to affirm that homosexuality (as the Catholic Church teaches) constitutes an objective disordering in the structure of human existence, and the fact that the Church is convinced that she does not have the right to confer priestly ordination on women is already seen by some as irreconcilable with the spirit of the European Constitution. I mention only some points here; I do not intend to provide an exhaustive list of the contents of this canon of the Enlightenment culture. It is obvious that it contains important values that are essential for us, precisely as Christians, and we do not wish to do without them. At the same time, it is equally obvious that the concept of liberty on which this culture is based inevitably leads to contradictions, since it is either badly defined or not defined at all. And it is clear that the very fact of employing this concept entails limitations on freedom that we could not even have imagined a generation ago. A confused ideology of liberty leads to a dogmatism that is proving ever more hostile to real liberty.

We must of course return to the question of the inherent contradictions in the form that the Enlightenment culture takes today; but first we must finish our description of it. Since it is the culture of a reason that has finally achieved complete self-awareness, it naturally boasts of its claimed universality and imagines that it is complete in itself, without needing any other cultural factors to complement it. We see these two characteristics clearly in the discussion of which states may join the European Community and, especially, in the debate about the potential entry of Turkey to this Community. Here we have a state, or perhaps better a cultural environment, that does not have Christian roots but has been influenced by Islamic culture. Ataturk attempted to transform Turkey into a laicist state, seeking to plant on Muslim soil the secular attitudes that had matured in the Christian world of Europe, and one may of course ask whether this is in fact possible. But according to the thesis of the laicist Enlightenment culture of Europe, it is only the norms and substance of this same Enlightenment culture that can determine the identity of Europe, and it follows that every state that accepts these criteria can belong to Europe. Ultimately, it is unimportant to know on *which* framework of roots this culture of liberty and democracy is planted. And we are told that this is precisely why the roots cannot be included in the definition of the bases of Europe—for these are dead roots that do not form part of today's identity. Accordingly, this new identity, which is defined exclusively by the Enlightenment culture, entails that God has nothing whatever to do with public life and with the foundations of the state.

This makes everything logical and even, in a certain sense, plausible. For what higher good could we wish than that democracy and human rights be respected everywhere? But at this point, we must ask whether this Enlightenment-laicist culture is truly the culture—finally revealed in all its universality—of a reason that is common to all men, a culture that must be accepted everywhere, even if it is rooted in a soil that is historically and culturally diverse. And one must ask whether this culture is truly complete in itself, so that it does not need any roots outside itself.

2

The Significance and Limits of Today's Rationalistic Culture

We must now investigate these two questions. The first asked whether we have at last achieved the philosophy that is universally valid and completely scientific, a philosophy in which the reason common to all men finds expression. We must begin by replying that we have undoubtedly made important gains that can claim a general validity: the assurance that religion cannot be imposed by the state but can only be accepted in liberty; the respect of the fundamental rights of man, which are equal for all; the separation of powers and the control of power. These are fundamental values, which we acknowledge to be generally valid; but we cannot imagine that they can be realized in the same manner in every historical context. The sociological presuppositions for a democracy based on political parties, as in the West, do not exist in every society, and in the great majority of historical contexts, the total religious neutrality of the state must be considered an illusion. This brings us to the problems raised by the second question; but let us first clear up the question of whether the modern philosophies inspired by the Enlightenment, taken as a whole, can be considered the last word of that reason which is common to all men. These philosophies are characterized by their positivist—and therefore anti-metaphysical—character, so that ultimately there is no place for God in them. They are based on a self-limitation of the positive reason that is adequate in the technological sphere but entails a mutilation of man if it is generalized. The result is that man no longer accepts any moral authority apart from his own calculations. As we have seen, even the concept of liberty, which initially seemed capable of expanding without any limits, leads in the end to the self-destruction of liberty itself. It is true that the positivist philosophies contain important elements of truth; but these are based on a self-limitation of reason that is typical of one determined cultural situation, that of the modern West, and, as such, certainly cannot be considered the last word of reason. Although they may seem totally rational, they are not in fact the voice of reason. They, too, have their cultural ties, since they are linked to the situation of the West today. This is why they are not that philosophy which one day could enjoy validity throughout the whole world.

Above all, however, we must affirm that this Enlightenment philosophy, with its related culture, is incomplete. It consciously cuts off its own historical roots, depriving itself of the powerful sources from which it sprang. It detaches itself from what we might call the basic memory of mankind, without which reason loses its orientation, for now the guiding principle is that man's capability determines what he does. If you know how to do something, then you are also permitted to do it; to know how to do something, but not be able to do it, is a state of affairs that no longer exists, since it would run counter to liberty—which is the absolute, supreme value. But man knows how to do many things, and this knowledge increases all the time. If this know-how does not find its criterion in a moral norm, it becomes a power for destruction, as we can already see in the world around us. Man knows how to clone human beings, and therefore he does so. Man knows how to use human beings as "storerooms" of organs for other men, and therefore he does so. He does so, because this seems something demanded by his own liberty. Man knows how to build atomic bombs, and therefore he makes them, and he is willing in principle to use them, too. Even terrorism is ultimately based on this modality of man's "self-authorization", not on the teachings of the Qur'an. The radical detachment of the Enlightenment philosophy from its roots ultimately leads it to dispense with man. The spokesmen of the natural sciences tell us that man basically does not possess any liberty—in total contradiction of the starting point of the whole question. The more advanced spokesmen of a philosophy that is clearly separated from the roots of the historical memory of humanity tell us that man ought not to imagine that he is something different from all other living beings. And it follows that man ought not to be treated any differently from them.

We asked two questions: whether the rationalistic (positivist) philosophy is strictly rational, and therefore universally valid, and whether it is complete. Is it enough on its own? May, or indeed must, it abandon its historical roots to the sphere of the dead past, that is, to the sphere of that which can claim no more than a subjective validity? Our answer to all these questions must be an unambiguous No. This philosophy expresses, not the complete reason of man, but only one part of it. And this mutilation of reason means that we cannot consider it to be rational at all. Hence, it is incomplete and can recover its health only through reestablishing contact with its roots. A tree without roots dries up . . .

In affirming this, we are not denying all the positive and important contributions of this philosophy. Rather, we are stating that it needs to be completed, since it is profoundly incomplete. And this brings us back to the two controversial points in the preamble to the European Constitution. The failure to mention Christian roots is not the expression of a superior tolerance that

43

respects all cultures in the same way and chooses not to accord privileges to any one of them. Rather, it expresses the absolutization of a way of thinking and living that is radically opposed (*inter alia*) to all the other historical cultures of humanity. The real antagonism typical of today's world is not that between diverse religious cultures; rather, it is the antagonism between the radical emancipation of man from God, from the roots of life, on the one hand, and the great religious cultures, on the other. If we come to experience a clash of cultures, this will not be due to a conflict between the great religions, which of course have always been at odds with one another but, nevertheless, have ultimately always understood how to coexist with one another. The coming clash will be between this radical emancipation of man and the great historical cultures. Accordingly, the refusal to refer to God in the Constitution is not the expression of a tolerance that wishes to protect the nontheistic religions and the dignity of atheists and agnostics; rather, it is the expression of a consciousness that would like to see God eradicated once and for all from the public life of humanity and shut up in the subjective sphere of cultural residues from the past. In this way, relativism, which is the starting point of this whole process, becomes a dogmatism that believes itself in possession of the definitive knowledge of human reason, with the right to consider everything else merely as a stage in human history that is basically obsolete and deserves to be relativized. In reality, this means that we have need of roots if we are to survive and that we must not lose sight of God if we do not want human dignity to disappear.

3

The Permanent Significance of the Christian Faith

Does this amount to a simple rejection of the Enlightenment and modernity? Certainly not! From the very beginning, Christianity has understood itself to be the religion of the *Logos*, to be a religion in keeping with reason. When it identified its forerunners, these were primarily, not in the other religions, but in that philosophical enlightenment which cleared the road from the various traditions that cluttered it in order to turn to the search for truth and to turn toward the good, toward the one God who is above all gods. As a religion of the persecuted, and as a universal religion that was wider than any one state or people, it denied the government the right to consider religion as part of the order of the state, thus stating the principle of the liberty of faith. It has always defined men—all men without distinction—as creatures of God, made in his image, proclaiming the principle that they are equal in dignity, though of course within the given limits of societal order. In this sense, the Enlightenment has a Christian origin, and it is not by chance that it was born specifically and exclusively within the sphere of the Christian faith, in places where Christianity, contrary to its own nature, had unfortunately become mere tradition and the religion of the state. Philosophy, as the investigation of the rational element (which includes the rational element in our faith), had always been a positive element in Christianity, but the voice of reason had become excessively tame. It was and remains the merit of the Enlightenment to have drawn attention afresh to these original Christian values and to have given reason back its own voice. In its Constitution on the Church the Modern World, the Second Vatican Council restated this profound harmony between Christianity and the Enlightenment, seeking to achieve a genuine reconciliation between the

Church and modernity, which is the great patrimony of which both parties must take care.

This means that both parties must reflect on their own selves and be ready to accept correction. Christianity must always remember that it is the religion of the *Logos.* Christianity is faith in the *Creator Spiritus,* from whom comes everything that is real. Precisely this ought to give Christianity its philosophical power today, since the problem is whether the world comes from an irrational source, so that reason would be nothing but a "by-product" (perhaps even a harmful by-product) of the development of the world, or whether the world comes from reason, so that its criterion and its goal is reason. The Christian faith opts for this second thesis and has good arguments to back it up, even from a purely philosophical point of view, despite the fact that so many people today consider the first thesis the only "rational" and modern view. A reason that has its origin in the irrational and is itself ultimately irrational does not offer a solution to our problems. Only that creative reason which has manifested itself as love in the crucified God can truly show us what life is.

The dialogue between those outside the Church and us Catholics, us Christians, is a matter of great urgency, and we must at all costs remain faithful to this basic principle of living a faith that proceeds from the *Logos*, from creative reason, and is therefore open to all that is truly rational. But at this point, speaking as a believer, I should like to make a proposal to those outside the Church. In the age of the Enlightenment, the attempt was made to understand and define the essential norms of morality by saying that these would be valid *etsi Deus non daretur*, even if God did not exist. In the situation of confessional antagonism and in the crisis that threatened the image of God, they tried to keep the essential moral values outside the controversies and to identify an evidential quality in these values that would make them independent of the many divisions and uncertainties of the various philosophies and religious confessions. The intention was to guarantee the bases of life in society and, in more general terms, the bases of humanity. At that time, this seemed possible, since the great fundamental convictions created by Christianity were largely resistant to attack and seemed undeniable. But that is no longer the case. The search for this kind of reassuring certainty, something that could go unchallenged despite all the disagreements, has not succeeded. Not even Kant's truly stupendous endeavors managed to create the necessary certainty that would be shared by all. Kant had denied that God could be known within the sphere of pure reason, but at the same time, he had presented God, freedom, and immortality as postulates of practical reason, without which he saw no coherent possibility of acting in a moral manner. I wonder if the situation of today's world might not make us return to the idea that Kant was right? Let me put this in different terms: the attempt, carried to extremes, to shape human affairs to the total exclusion of God leads us more and more to the brink of the abyss, toward the utter annihilation of man. We must therefore reverse the axiom of the Enlightenment and say: Even the one who does not succeed in finding the path to accepting the existence of God ought nevertheless to try to live and to direct his life *veluti si Deus daretur,* as if God did indeed exist. This is the advice Pascal gave to his non-believing friends, and it is the advice that I should like to give to our friends today who do not believe. This does not impose limitations on anyone's freedom; it gives support to all our human affairs and supplies a criterion of which human life stands sorely in need.

Our greatest need in the present historical moment is people who make God credible in this world by means of the enlightened faith they live. The negative testimony of Christians who spoke of God but lived in a manner contrary to him has obscured the image of God and has opened the doors to disbelief.

We need men who keep their eyes fixed on God, learning from him what true humanity means.

We need men whose intellect is enlightened by the light of God, men whose hearts are opened by God, so that their intellect can speak to the intellect of others and their hearts can open the hearts of others. It is only by means of men who have been touched by God that God can return to be with mankind.

We need men like Benedict of Nursia, who, in an age of dissipation and decadence, immersed himself in the uttermost solitude. Then, after all the purifications he had to undergo, he succeeded in rising again to the light. He returned and made his foundation at Monte Cassino, the "city on the hill" where, in the midst of so many ruins, he assembled the forces from which a new world was formed. In this way, like Abraham, Benedict became the father of many peoples. The recommendations to his monks with which he concludes his *Rule* show us, too, the path that leads on high, away from the crises and the ruins:

> Just as there is an evil zeal of bitterness which separates from God and leads to hell, so is there is a good zeal which separates from evil and leads to God and life everlasting.
>
> Let monks, therefore, exercise this zeal with the most fervent love. Let them, that is, give one another precedence. Let them bear with the greatest patience one another's infirmities, whether of body or of character. . . . Let them practice fraternal charity with a pure love. Let them fear God. . . . Let them prefer nothing whatever to Christ. And may he bring us all alike to life everlasting.[1]

[1] Saint Benedict, *the Rule of Saint Benedict*, trans. Justin McCann, O.S.B. (London: Sheed and Ward, 1976), chap. 72.

THE RIGHT TO LIFE

I

Why We Must Not Give Up the Fight

One widespread section of public opinion in the educated bourgeoisie may find it exaggerated and inopportune—indeed, downright distasteful—that we continue to remind them that the problem of respect for a life that has been conceived and is not yet born is a decisive question. In the last fifteen years, almost all Western countries have legalized abortion, to the accompaniment of lacerating debates; ought we not today to consider this problem settled and avoid brushing the dust off antagonistic ideological positions that have been made obsolete by the course of events? Why not accept that we have lost this battle and choose instead to dedicate our energies to initiatives that can hope to find support in a broader social consensus? Indeed, if we remain on the superficial level, we could be convinced that the legal approval of abortion has not really changed much in our private lives and in the life of our societies; basically, everything seems to be going on as before. Everyone can act in accordance with his conscience: a woman who does not want to have an abortion is not compelled to do so, and a woman who does have an abortion with the approval of a law would perhaps have done so in any case (or so we are told). It all takes place in the silence of an operating room, which at least guarantees that this "medical intervention" will take place with a certain degree of safety: and it is as if the fetus that will never see the light of day had in fact never existed. Who notices what is going on? Why should we continue to speak publicly of this drama? Is it not perhaps better to leave it buried in the silence of the consciences of the individuals involved?

The Book of Genesis contains a passage that addresses our problem with impressive eloquence: the blessing the Lord God pronounces on Noah and his sons after the flood. After the event of sin, God reestablishes here, once and for all, the only laws that can guarantee the continuation of life for the human race. The disorder and degeneration that followed the fall of our first parents have left their mark on the creation that God's hands had made absolutely perfect. Violence and an unending chain of reciprocal killings have spread through the world, making impossible the peace of a social life ordered in keeping with the principles of justice. Now, after the great purification of the flood, God lays aside the bow of his wrath and embraces the world anew in his mercy, indicating (in view of the future redemption) the essential norms for the world's survival: "For your lifeblood I will surely require a reckoning; of every beast I will require it and of man; of every man's brother I will require the life of man. Whoever sheds the blood of man, by man shall his blood be shed; for God made man in his own image" (Gen 9:5–6).

With these words, God claims the life of man as his own specific possession: it remains under his direct and immediate protection. It is something "sacred". When a man's blood is shed, it cries out to him (Gen 4:10), because man is made in his image and likeness. The authority of society and the authorities in society are instituted by him precisely in order to guarantee the respect of this fundamental right, which is endangered by the wicked heart of man.

It follows that the recognition of the sacred character of human life and of its inviolability—a principle admitting no exceptions—is not some trivial little problem or a question that may be considered relative, in view of the pluralism of opinions we find in modern society. The text from Genesis guides our reflections in a double sense, which corresponds well to the double dimension of the questions we asked at the beginning of this essay:

First, there are no "small murders". The respect of every human life is an essential condition if a societal life worthy of the name is to be possible.

Secondly, when man's conscience loses respect for life as something sacred, he inevitably ends by losing his own identity.

2

The Law of the Jungle, the Rule of Law

In today's pluralistic societies, where various religious, cultural, and ideological orientations coexist, it is becoming ever more difficult to guarantee a common basis of ethical values shared by all and capable of providing a sufficient foundation for democracy itself. Very many people are, indeed, convinced that we cannot do without a minimum of moral values that are recognized and sanctioned in social life; but the substance of such values increasingly evaporates the more we struggle to attain the consensus they must obtain on the level of society. One single value seems not to be the object of discussion, since it is indisputable and has therefore become a filter through which every other "value" is passed, namely, the right of the individual to express himself freely, without any impositions from outside himself, at least so long as his freedom does not infringe the rights of others.

This is how the right to abortion is invoked as a constitutive element in the right to liberty on the part of the woman, the man, and society itself. The woman has the right to continue her professional work, to safeguard her reputation, to maintain a certain standard of life. The man has the right to decide about his life-style, to pursue a career, to enjoy the fruits of his work. Society has the right to control the numerical level of the population, in order to guarantee its citizens a widespread prosperity through a balanced management of resources, of work, and so on. All these rights are real and well founded. No one denies that the concrete existential situation in which the decision is reached to have an abortion can sometimes be dramatic. Nevertheless, it is a fact that this claim to exercise real rights is demanded to the detriment of the life of an innocent human being whose rights are not even taken into consideration. In this way, one becomes blind to the right to life of another, the smallest and weakest person involved, one without a voice. The rights of *some* individuals are affirmed at the cost of the fundamental right to life of *another* individual. This is why every legalization of abortion implies the idea that law is based on power.

Mostly, this happens inadvertently; nevertheless, it poses a real threat to the very foundations of an authentic democracy based on a stable ordering of justice. The constitutional charters of the Western countries, which are the fruit of a complex process of cultural maturation and of struggles that lasted for centuries, are based on the idea of a stable ordering of justice and on the consciousness that all who share a common humanity are fundamentally equal. At the same time, these documents express an awareness of the profound iniquity that exists when the real but secondary interests of some persons prevail over the fundamental rights of others. The Universal Declaration of Human Rights, signed by almost all the countries of the world in 1948 in the aftermath of the terrible ordeal of the Second World War, expresses fully (even in its title) the awareness that human rights—the most fundamental of which is, of course, the right to life itself—belong to man *by nature*; that the state *recognizes* them but does not in fact confer them; and that they are applicable to *all* men as such, not because of other *secondary* characteristics of particular individuals, which others would be entitled to define at their pleasure. It follows that a state that claims the prerogative of defining who is and who is not the subject of rights, and that consequently accepts that some persons have the right to violate the fundamental right to life of other persons, contradicts the democratic ideal, although it continues to appeal to this claim. Such a state imperils the very basis on which it governs. For when it accepts that the rights of the weakest may be violated, it also accepts that the law of the jungle prevails over the rule of law.

3

We Must Use Our Eyes!

In addition to the legal problem, on a more fundamental level we have the moral problem that passes through the *heart* of each one of us, in that hidden interior room where our freedom decides for good or evil. I have said that, when the decision is taken in favor of abortion, there is necessarily a moment at which one agrees to shut one's eyes to the right to life of the little one who has just been conceived. The moral drama, the decision for good or evil, begins with our eyes, when we choose whether or not to look at the face of the other. Why is infanticide almost unanimously rejected today, whereas we have become virtually inured to abortion? Perhaps the only reason is that in the case of abortion, one does not see the face of the one condemned never to see the light of day. Many psychologists have pointed out that in women who intend to have an abortion, the spontaneous pictures formed in the imagination of a pregnant woman are suppressed. These imaginative speculations —what name will the child have, what will it look like, what will its future be?—often return later as unresolved feelings of guilt to torment the conscience.

The face of the other addresses an appeal to my liberty, asking me to welcome him and take care of him, asking me to affirm his value per se, not merely to the extent to which he may happen to coincide with my own interests. The moral truth, in this case the truth of the unique and unrepeatable value of this person made in the image of God, is a truth that makes demands of my liberty. When I decide to look him in the face, I am deciding on conversion, I am resolving to let the other address his appeal to me, to go beyond the confines of my own self and to make space for him. This is why even the evidential character of this moral value depends to a large extent on a secret decision by my liberty to agree to look at the other and thus be provoked to change my life.

In his preface to the well-known book by the French biologist Jacques Testart, *L'Œuf transparent,* the philosopher Michel Serres (who seems not to be a believer) takes up the question of the respect due to the human embryo and asks: "Who is man?" He points out that philosophy and culture do not supply unambiguous and genuinely satisfactory answers, but he notes that although we do not have a precise theoretical definition of man, we know perfectly well in our experience of everyday life who man is. We know this above all when we are confronted by someone who is suffering, by someone who is a victim of power, by someone who is defenseless and condemned to death: "*Ecce homo!*" Yes, this non-believer quotes the words of Pontius Pilate, who possessed the plenitude of power, in the presence of Jesus, who had been stripped, scourged, and crowned with thorns and was now condemned to die on the Cross. Who is man? It is precisely the one who is most weak and defenseless, the one who has neither power nor a voice to defend himself, the one whom we may pass by in the course of life, pretending not to see him.

The one against whom we may close our heart, saying that he never existed.

We are at once reminded of another page in the Gospels, which offered a reply to a similar request for a definition: "And who is my neighbor?" We know that, if we are to recognize who our neighbor is, we must agree to become his neighbor, and that means stopping, getting down from our horse, drawing near to the one who is in need, and taking care of him. "As you did it to one of the least of these my brethren, you did it to me" (Mt 25:40).

I should like to draw attention to a passage by a great Italian-German thinker, Romano Guardini:

> Man is not inviolable merely in virtue of the fact that he exists. An animal, too, could lay claim to such a right, since it, too, exists. . . . Man's life remains inviolable because *he is a person.* . . . To be a person is not a psychological but an existential fact: it does not depend fundamentally on one's age or psychological condition or on the gifts of nature with which the subject is provided. . . . The personality may remain below the threshold of consciousness—for example, when we are sleeping—but it remains, nevertheless, and must be taken into account. The personality may

as yet be undeveloped—for example, when we are children—but it has a claim to moral respect from the very beginning. It is even possible that the personality in general may not emerge in one's acts, since the psycho-physical presuppositions are lacking—as in those who are mentally ill. . . . Finally, the personality can also remain hidden—as in the embryo—but it exists in the embryo from the outset and has its own rights. It is this personality that gives men their dignity. It distinguishes them from material objects and makes them *subjects*. . . . We treat a thing like a thing when we possess it, use it, and finally destroy it—or, if we are speaking of human beings, kill it. *The prohibition against taking human life expresses in the most acute form the prohibition of treating a man as if he were a thing.*[1]

This makes it clear that the look I freely direct to the other is decisive for my own dignity, too. I can acquiesce in reducing the other to a thing that I use and destroy; but by the same token, I must accept the consequences of the way I use my eyes here. These consequences fall back on my own head: "You will yourselves be measured by the measure with which you measure." The way I look at the other is decisive for my own humanity. I can treat him quite simply like a

[1] From "I diritti del nascituro", *Studi cattolici*, May/June, 1974.

thing, forgetting my dignity and his, forgetting that both he and I are made in the image and likeness of God. The other is the custodian of my own dignity. This is why morality, which begins with this look directed to the other, is the custodian of the truth and the dignity of man: man needs morality in order to be himself and not lose his dignity in the world of things.

There is one last decisive step that we must take in our reflections, a step that brings us back to the passage in Genesis where we began. How is it possible for a man to use his eyes in such a way that he perceives and respects the dignity of the other person and guarantees his own dignity? The drama of our times consists precisely in our incapacity to look at ourselves like this— and that is why we find it threatening to look at the other and must protect ourselves against this. In reality, morality is always embedded in a wider religious context in which it "breathes" and finds its proper environment. Outside this environment, morality cannot breathe; it weakens and then dies. The ethical recognition of the sacred character of life and the commitment to ensure the respect for life require a context and a perspective, and these are supplied by faith in creation. A child can open himself confidently to love if he knows he is loved, and he can develop and grow if he knows that he is followed everywhere by his parents' look of love. Similarly, we too succeed in looking at others in a manner that respects their personal dignity if we experience how God looks at us in love. It is this look that reveals to us how precious is our person. "Then God said, 'Let us make man in our image, after our likeness.'. . . And God saw everything that he had made, and behold, it was very good" (Gen 1:26, 31).

Christianity is this remembrance of the look of love that the Lord directs to man, this look that preserves the fullness of his truth and the ultimate guarantee of his dignity. The mystery of Christmas reminds us that in the Christ who is born, every human life—from the very beginning—is definitively blessed and welcomed by the look of God's mercy. Christians know this and stand with their own life under this look of love; with this look, they receive a message that is essential for man's life and for his future. This means that they can humbly *and* proudly accept today the task of proclaiming the good news of the faith, without which human existence cannot long survive. In this task of announcing the dignity of man and the duties of respecting life that flow from this dignity, they know they will probably meet derision and hatred. But the world cannot live without them.

I should like to conclude with the stupendous words of the ancient *Letter to Diognetus*, which describes the absolutely essential mission of Christians in the world:

> For Christians are not distinct from other men in terms either of their territories, their language, or their way of life. . . . They live in the cities of the Greeks or the barbarians, as the lot has fallen to each one, and they adapt to the customs of the place in their clothing and food and in the rest of their way of living, offering the example of their marvelous form of social life, which all admit has something incredible about it. They live each in his own native land, but as if they were foreigners. They take their share in all the burdens, as citizens, and they put up with everything, as strangers. Every foreign land is a native land for them, and every native land is a foreign land. They get married like everyone else and have children, but they do not expose their newborn children. They share their table, but not their

bed. They live in the flesh, but not according to
the flesh. They dwell on earth, but they are citizens of heaven. They obey the laws that have
been laid down, but with their manner of life
they rise above the laws. They love all and are
persecuted by all. . . . To put it in a word, Christians are in the world what the soul is in the
body. . . . The soul loves the flesh that hates it and
loves its limbs: Christians, too, love those who
hate them. The soul is shut up within the body,
but it is the soul that sustains the body: Christians, too, are held in the world as in a prison, but
it is they who sustain the world. . . . God has
assigned them such a high position, and they are
not allowed to abandon it.

WHAT DOES IT MEAN
TO BELIEVE?

Faith is the fundamental act of Christian existence.

The essential structure of Christianity finds expression in the act of faith, which is the answer it gives to the question: How can we attain our destiny and thereby realize our humanity? There are of course other answers. Not all religions are a "faith". For example, Buddhism in its classical form does not at all tend toward this act of self-transcendence, of encounter with the one who is totally other, with this God who speaks to me or who summons me to love. Instead, Buddhism is characterized by an act of radical internalization, not an act that makes one emerge from oneself, but an act of returning into oneself. This act is meant to lead to liberation from the yoke of individuality, from the burden represented by the fact of being a person, to a return into the common unity of being. Compared with the experience we have of being, we can describe the absolute otherness of *this* "being" as non-being, as nothing.

Faith and Everyday Life:
A Fundamental Human Attitude

It is not my intention to enter this particular discussion. What interests us for the moment is, put very simply, how to understand the fundamental act of Christian existence, the act of faith. As soon as we set out on this path of reflection, we encounter a difficulty, since we must ask: Is faith truly an attitude worthy of a modern adult? "Believing" seems a provisional, transitory stage that ought in the last analysis to be left behind . . . although this is often inevitable in our life, precisely because we are speaking here of a provisional attitude. No one is truly capable of possessing a personal knowledge and mastery of all those realities on which our daily life in a technological civilization is based. We are obliged to accept an enormous number of things, in most cases putting our trust in "science"—and all the more so, because the experience we have in common seems a sufficient confirmation of this trust. All of us, to a greater or lesser degree, make use of the products of technology, although we are ignorant of its scientific foundations: Which of us can calculate or verify the statics of a building? Which of us knows how an elevator works—to say nothing of the worlds of electricity and electronics, which are so familiar to us? And how far— to move onto a much more delicate subject— can we trust the information on the packaging of a pharmaceutical compound? We could multiply examples. . . . We live within a network of unknown quantities, with the general expectation that these will provide us with positive experiences. We believe that all this is not unfounded, and this kind of "faith" allows us to enjoy the benefits of other people's professional knowledge.

But what kind of faith is this, which we practice all the time without even noticing and which is at the basis of the life we share every day? Without at once trying to offer a definition, let us begin on the level of what is immediately observable. Two contrasting aspects of this kind of "faith" strike us at once. First of all, we can affirm that a faith of this kind is indispensable in our life. This is true for the simple reason that, if this were not the case, nothing would function any more: each one of us would have to start afresh all the time. This is also true on a deeper level, in the sense that human life becomes impossible if one can no longer trust the other and others, if one cannot rely a priori on their experience and knowledge and on what they offer us. This is one of the positive aspects of this "faith". On the other hand, of course, it is the expression of an ignorance that makes the best of a bad job: it would undeniably be better if we did possess the appropriate knowledge.

We have elaborated here what we might call an "axiological structure" of this natural faith. We have examined the values it contains and seen that such a faith is a lesser value than "knowledge" but at the same time a foundational value of human existence. Without this basis, no society could survive. We can also identify the various elements involved in the "structure of action" of such a faith. These are three in number. First, this faith always refers to someone who possesses up-to-date knowledge of the question: it presupposes that qualified and credible persons do in fact possess this knowledge. The second element is the trust on the part of the "multitude" of those who, in the daily use they make of things, do not rely on the solid knowledge that actually produced them. Finally, the third element we must mention is the existence of a kind of verification of knowledge in daily experience. I am not capable of verifying scientifically whether the act of switching on a reading lamp is the result of a process based on the principles of electricity, but this does not lead me to reject the affirmation that this is in fact the case, because my household appliances function in daily life, despite my own lack of professional knowledge.

This means that although I may not have been initiated into this knowledge, nevertheless I am not acting in a pure "faith" bereft of any kind of confirmation.

2

Can Agnosticism Be a Solution?

All this opens up perspectives on religious faith and allows us to discern some structural analogies; but as soon as we attempt to pass to this level, we encounter an objection that has a certain weight and could be formulated as follows. It may, indeed, be true that within the network of human relationships it is impossible for each individual to "know" everything that is necessary and useful for life and that, therefore, our possibilities for action are based on the fact that we ourselves participate by "faith" in the "knowledge" of others. Nevertheless, we remain all the time within the sphere of a human knowledge that is always in principle accessible to all men. When, however, we speak of faith in revelation, we pass beyond the boundaries of that knowledge which is typical of human life. Even if the hypothesis be granted that the existence of God could become an object of "knowledge", at least revelation and its contents would remain an object of "faith" for each one of us, something that surpasses those realities that are accessible to our knowledge. Consequently, in this field there is no one in whom we could put our trust or to whose specialist knowledge we could refer, since no one could have a direct knowledge of such realities on the basis of his own personal studies. This means that we are confronted once again, and in an even more urgent fashion, with the problem: Is *this* type of faith compatible with modern critical knowledge? Would it not be more appropriate for an adult of our times to refrain from expressing judgments on such matters and to wait for the day when science will have definitive answers even to this kind of question?

The attitude revealed in this way of putting the problem is undoubtedly that of the average person with a university education today: intellectual honesty and humility in the face of the unknown seem to recommend agnosticism rather than an explicit atheism, since the latter, too, claims to know too much about these things and clearly has a dogmatic element of its own. No one can claim to "know", strictly speaking, that God does not exist. One can at most take his non-existence as a working hypothesis, on the basis of which one then tries to explain the universe. Modern science basically takes this line. Nevertheless, this kind of methodological approach is aware of its limitations: clearly, it is never possible to get beyond the sphere of the hypothetical. No matter how evident an atheistic interpretation of the universe may appear, it will never lead to the scientific certainty that God does not exist. No one can carry out experiments on the totality of existence or its preconditions. This brings us in a very straightforward manner to the unsurpassable limits inherent in the "human condition" and in man's capacity for knowledge *qua* man, that is, not merely with regard to his present-day circumstances, but in terms of his very essence. Of its nature, the question of God cannot forcibly be made an object of scientific research in the strict sense of that term, and this means that the declaration of "scientific atheism" is an absurd claim—yesterday, today, or tomorrow. This, however, makes it all the more urgent to know whether the question of God does surpass the limits of human capabilities as such, so that agnosticism would in fact be the only correct attitude for man: the acknowledgment, appropriate and honest, "devout" in the profound meaning of that word, of that which eludes our grasp and our field of vision, a reverence vis-à-vis something that is inaccessible to us. Might not this be the new form of intellectual devotion: to leave aside whatever lies beyond our grasp and be content with what we are permitted to know?

An authentic believer who wishes to reply to this question must be on his guard against an unreflecting haste. This type of humility and devotion calls forth at once an objection: Is it not perhaps the case that the thirst for the infinite is a fundamental aspect of human nature? Is not, indeed, this thirst the very essence of human nature? Its only limit can be that which is illimitable, and the limits of science must not be confused with the limits of our existence as such, for that would be a failure to comprehend either science or man. If science were to claim to exhaust the limits of human knowledge, it would end up by denying its own scientific character. All this seems to me undoubtedly true, but as a reply it is (as I have said) premature. We ought rather to examine patiently the plausibility of the hypothesis of agnosticism and see whether it can hold up as a response not only to science, but also to human life.

The true way to call agnosticism into question is to ask whether its program can be realized. Is it possible for us, as human beings, purely and simply to lay aside the question of God, that is, the question of our origin, of our final destiny, and of the measure of our existence? Can we be content to live under the hypothetical formula "as if God did not exist", while it is possible that he does in fact exist? The question of God is not a merely theoretical problem for man, like, for example, the problem of knowing whether there exist other elements, as yet unknown, outside the periodic table. On the contrary, the question of God is an eminently practical problem with consequences in every sphere of our lives. Even if I throw in my theoretical lot with agnosticism,

I am nevertheless compelled in practice to choose between two alternatives: either to live as if God did not exist or else to live as if God did exist and was the decisive reality of my existence. If I act according to the first alternative, I have in practice adopted an atheistic position and have made a hypothesis (which may also be false) the basis of my entire life. If I decide for the second option, I remain here, too, in the sphere of a purely human belief, and one can certainly recall in this context the proposal made by Pascal, whose philosophical controversy, at the dawn of the modern age, dealt with this problem. Having reached the conviction that the question could not in reality be resolved by means of thought alone, he recommended that the agnostic risk taking the second option and live as if God existed. According to Pascal, it is in the course of experience, and only thanks to experience, that at some point the agnostic will recognize the correctness of his choice.

Let us leave this question here; it is clear that the prestige enjoyed by the agnostic solution today does not stand up to closer examination. As a pure theory, it may seem exceedingly illuminating. But in its essence, agnosticism is much more than a theory: what is at stake here is the praxis of one's life. When one attempts to "put it into practice" in one's real field of action, agnosticism slips out of one's hands like a soap bubble; it dissolves into thin air, because it is not possible to escape the very option it seeks to avoid. When faced with the question of God, man cannot permit himself to remain neutral. All he can say is Yes or No—without ever avoiding all the consequences that derive from this choice even in the smallest details of life. Accordingly, we see that the question of God is ineluctable; one is not permitted to abstain from casting one's vote. Obviously, however, the conditions relevant to the knowledge of God are necessarily of a particular kind. In this question, we are not analyzing isolated fragments of reality that we might in some way take into our hands, verify experientially, and then master. This question regards, not that which is below us, but that which is above us. It regards, not something we could dominate, but that which exercises its lordship over us and over the whole of reality. Even when I encounter another person, I am not capable with a single glance of penetrating the depths of his character and the vast expanses of his spirit in the same way I can examine a piece of matter or some other living organism. How much less will I be able to approach the very foundation of the universe in this manner!

This does not mean that we have now entered the sphere of the irrational. On the contrary, what we are looking for is the very foundation of all rationality; we are inquiring into how its light can be perceived. To explain this point in detail, much more time would be required than is available for one single lecture. But there is one fundamental point that seems obvious to me: where *everything*, and the foundations of everything, are involved, the one who endeavors to comprehend is inevitably challenged to get involved with the *totality* of his being, with all the faculties of perception he has been given. And his search for knowledge must aim not only to collect a large number of individual details, but (as far as is possible) to grasp the totality as such. We can also affirm that there are some fundamental human attitudes that are indispensable methodological presuppositions for the knowledge of God. These include: listening to the message that is brought to us by our own existence and by the world in general; a vigilant attentiveness vis-à-vis the discoveries and the religious experience of humanity; and the decisive and persevering employment of our time and our internal energy on this problem, which concerns each one of us personally.

3

The Natural Knowledge of God

We must now inquire whether there is an answer to such a question for man; and if so, what kind of certainty we are allowed to attain.

In his Letter to the Romans, the apostle Paul found himself confronted precisely with these problems, and he responded with a philosophical reflection based on facts presented by the history of religions. In the megalopolis of Rome, the Babylon of that age, he encountered the type of moral decadence that comes from the total loss of tradition: people were deprived of that interior evidential character that in other times had been offered to man from the outset of his life by usages and customs. Where nothing can be taken for granted, everything becomes possible, and nothing is impossible any longer.

Now there is no value capable of sustaining man, and there are no inviolable norms. All that counts is man's ego and the present moment. The traditional religions are merely comfortable façades, without any spirituality; all that remains is a naked and crude cynicism. The apostle offers a surprising response to this metaphysical and moral cynicism of a decadent society dominated only by the law of the jungle. He declares that, in reality, this society knows God very well: "What can be known about God is plain to them" (Rom 1:19). He then backs up this affirmation: "Ever since the creation of the world his invisible nature, namely, his eternal power and deity, has been clearly perceived in the things that have been made" (1:20). And Paul draws the conclusion: "So they are without excuse" (1:20). According to the apostle, the truth is accessible to them, but they do not want it, because they refuse the demands that the truth would make on them. In this context, he says that they "by their wickedness suppress the truth" (1:18). Man resists the truth that would demand a submission expressed in giving glory and thanks to God (1:21). For Paul, the moral decadence of society is nothing more than the logical consequence and the faithful reflection of this radical perversion. When man prefers his own egoism, his pride, and his convenience to the demands made on him by the truth, the only possible outcome is an upside-down existence. Adoration is due to God alone, but what is adored is no longer God; images, outward appearances, and current opinion have dominion over man. This general alteration extends to every sphere of life. That which is against nature becomes the norm; the man who lives against the truth also lives against nature. His creativity is no longer at the service of the good: he devotes his genius to ever more refined forms of evil. The bonds between man and woman, and between parents and children, are dissolved, so that the very sources from which life springs are blocked up. It is no longer life that reigns, but death. A civilization of death is formed (Rom 1:21–32). The description of decadence that Paul sketches here astonishes us modern readers by its contemporary relevance.

However, he is not content merely to describe this state of affairs. There were many who did so in his days, and they display a perverse form of moralism that ends in taking pleasure precisely in the negative behavior it condemns. On the contrary, the apostle's analysis leads to a diagnosis and, hence, takes the form of a moral appeal: at the origin of all these negative things lies the negation of the truth in favor of what is convenient—or rather, of what is profitable. The starting point in man is a resistance to the evidential character of the Creator that is present in his heart as the sign of a Being who looks at him and summons him. Paul is far from regarding atheism, or an agnosticism that is lived out as atheism, as an innocent position. In his eyes, it is always the fruit of a refusal of that knowledge which is in fact offered to man; man is unwilling to accept the conditions attached to this knowledge. Man is not condemned to remain in uncertainty about God. He can "see" him, if he listens to the voice of God's Being and to the voice of his creation and lets himself be guided by this. Paul knows nothing of an atheism governed by purely idealistic motives.

What are we to say to this? Clearly, the apostle is playing in this passage on the contradiction between philosophy and religion that existed in antiquity. Greek philosophy had arrived at the knowledge of the one single foundation of the universe, the Spirit who alone is worthy of the name of "god", even if this knowledge existed in contradictory forms and was insufficiently detailed. But the energy that had sustained its critique of religion soon cooled down, and although this critical attitude was in fact an essential element in Greek philosophy, it increasingly turned to the justification of the worship of the gods and of the adoration of state power. It was therefore an obvious fact that "the truth" was "kept a prisoner". In this sense, Paul's diagnosis is well founded, when we bear in mind the historical situation he is addressing.

But despite this, can we really say that his affirmations possess a value that goes beyond this specific historical constellation? Certainly, we would need to modify the details. Nevertheless, Paul's words are essentially painting the picture, not of some particular historical situation, but of the permanent situation of humanity, of man, vis-à-vis God. The history of religions is coextensive with the history of humanity. As far as we know, there has never been an epoch in which the question of the One who is totally other, the Divine, has been alien to man. The knowledge of God has always existed. And everywhere in the history of religions, in various forms, we encounter the significant conflict between the knowledge of the one God and the attraction of other powers that are considered more dangerous or nearer at hand and, therefore, more important for man than the God who is distant and mysterious. All of history bears the traces of this strange dilemma between the non-violent, tranquil demands made by the truth, on the one hand, and the pressure brought to make profits and the need to have a good relationship with the powers that determine daily life by their interventions, on the other hand. Again and again, we see the victory of profit over truth, although the signs of the truth and of its own power never disappear completely. Indeed, they continue to live, often in surprising forms, in the very heart of a jungle full of poisonous plants.

But is this true even today, in a totally non-religious culture, in a culture of rationality and of the technology it harnesses? I believe that the answer is Yes. For even today, the question man poses inevitably goes beyond the sphere of technological rationality. Even today, we do not limit ourselves to the question: "What can I do?" We also ask: "What ought I to do, and who am I?" There are of course cosmological evolutionist systems that elevate the non-existence of God to the level of an obvious truth of reason and claim thereby to demonstrate that the truth is precisely that there is no God. But this type of general theory of knowledge betrays its own methodological character in essential points: the enormous gaps in our knowledge are filled by a series of mythological "theatrical props" with a fictitious rationality that will not deceive anyone. It is an obvious fact that the rational character of the universe cannot be explained *rationally* on the basis of something irrational! This is why the *Logos* that is at the origin of all things remains more than ever the best hypothesis, although this is of course a hypothesis that demands that we give up a position where it is we who are in charge and that we take the risk of assuming the position of humble listeners. Even in our days, we cannot say that the tranquil evidential character of God has been eliminated; but we must admit that it has been made more than ever unrecognizable by the violence that power and profit inflict on us. In this way, the contemporary situation is fundamentally marked by that same tension between opposite tendencies which runs through the whole of history. On the one side, there is the interior opening up of the human soul to God; but on the other side, there is the stronger attraction of our needs and our immediate experiences. Man is the battlefield where these two contend with each other. He is not capable of sloughing off God completely, nor does he have the strength to set out on the journey toward him. On his own, he is not capable of constructing a bridge that could establish a concrete relationship with this God. We can continue to affirm, with Saint Thomas, that unbelief is contrary to nature, but we must at once add that man is not able to clear up wholly the strange chiaroscuro that weighs down the questions concerning the eternal realities. If a genuine relationship is to come into existence, God must take the initiative: it is he who must come to meet man and address him.

4

"Supernatural" Faith and Its Origins

But how can this take place? This question takes us back to our initial reflections on the structure of faith, since our reply consists of the affirmation that the Word of God reaches us through the mediation of men who have heard it and touched it; men for whom God has become a concrete experience; men who know him at first hand, so to speak. In order to grasp this, we must reflect on the structure of knowledge and faith, which we set out above. We said that while faith has the character of a non-autonomous knowledge, at the same time it involves a factor of mutual trust whereby the knowledge of the other becomes my own knowledge. Hence, this factor of trust contains an element of participation: by means of my act of trust, I become a sharer in the knowledge of another. This is what we might call the social aspect of the phenomenon of faith. No one knows everything, but all of us together know what it is necessary to know; faith constitutes a network of reciprocal dependence that at the same time is a network of mutual solidarity, where each one sustains the other and is sustained by him. This fundamental anthropological structure can also be seen in our relationship with God, where it finds its original form and its integrating center.

Our knowledge of God is essentially based on this reciprocity, on a trust that becomes participation and is subsequently verified in the experience of each individual's life. The relationship with God is also, and indeed before all else, a relationship with men; it is based on a communion among men. We can also say that the communication that is specific to the relationship with God confers its most radical potential on human communication, raising it from the level of utilitarian interest to that level which is fundamental for the person.

If I am to accept as my own this knowledge of others that I am offered, and to experience its

reality in my personal life, it is of course necessary that I myself should be open to God. The
voice of the Eternal can reach me through the
mediation of the other person only if there is
in me an organ capable of receiving it. In this
sense, the shared knowledge of God that comes
to me from others is more personal than the
knowledge I share with the technician or specialist. The knowledge of God requires an interior vigilance, a spirituality, and an openness
of the heart that becomes personally aware, in
silence and recollection, that there exists a direct
access to the Creator. Nevertheless, it is true that
God does not disclose himself to an isolated ego.
God does not accept a merely individualistic
exclusiveness: our relationship to him is linked
to our brothers and sisters.

At this point, an unexpected path opens up
before us. We have said that what we call "natural faith", by which we trust results that we
cannot verify on our own, finds its justification
in the knowledge of those who are familiar
with the subject in general or who have themselves examined one specific question. Although
such a "faith" retains for the one involved its

character as faith, it appeals nevertheless to what another has *seen*. When we spoke of the religious question at the beginning of this lecture, it appeared that precisely this decisive element was lacking in supernatural-religious faith—that, at least, was the initial impression. Here there is no one who *sees* how things are, and it seems that we are never anything else but believers. This seemed to be the core of the problem of religious faith; but now we must say that that impression was misleading. In supernatural faith, too, there are a multitude who live from a small number of persons: and this small number lives for the multitude. Similarly, in the things of God we are not *all* like blind people who grope their way forward in the dark. Here, too, there are persons who are permitted *to see*: Christ says of the father of the great family of Israel, "Abraham . . . *saw* [my day] and was glad" (Jn 8:56). Christ is there, at the very center of history, as the great man who sees, and all his words flow from his immediate contact with the Father. As for us, the word that refers to our situation is: "He who has seen *me* has seen the Father" (Jn 14:9). In its innermost essence, the Christian faith is a participation in this act whereby Jesus *sees*. His act of seeing makes possible his word, which is the authentic expression of what he sees. Accordingly, what Jesus sees is the point of reference for our faith, the specific place where it is anchored.

5

Development of Premises

These fundamental premises imply a series of consequences I should like to develop briefly.

1. Faith is anchored in what Jesus and the
   saints see

Jesus, he who knows God directly, *sees* him. This is why he is the true mediator between God and man. His human act of seeing the divine reality is the source of light for all men. Nevertheless, we must not regard Jesus himself as one totally isolated, pushing him back into a remote historical past. We have already spoken of Abraham; let us now add that the light of Jesus is reflected in the saints and shines out through them. But the "saints" are not only those persons who have been explicitly canonized. There are always hidden saints, too, who receive in their communion with Jesus a ray of his splendor, a concrete and real experience of God.

To spell out what this fact means, we can perhaps take up a mysterious expression that the Old Testament uses when it tells the story of Moses: even if it is not possible to see him fully face to face, he nevertheless *sees* God, for he sees at least "his back" (Ex 33:23). And just as Moses' face shone after this encounter with God, so the light of Jesus shines forth through the life of these men. Saint Thomas Aquinas begins with this affirmation in his demonstration of the scientific character of theology. We should note that (according to Aristotle) all the sciences are interrelated within a system of reciprocal explanation and dependence. None of the sciences demonstrates or reflects everything; each of them, in one way or another, presupposes justifications that it originally draws from some other science. For Aristotle, there is only one science that penetrates to the genuine foundations of all human knowledge, and this is why he calls it the "first philosophy". All the other sciences presuppose at least this fundamental reflection and are therefore *scientiae subalternatae* (subaltern sciences) constructed on one or more other sciences.

Saint Thomas inserts his explanation of theology into this general theory of science. He says that, in this sense, theology, too, is a "subaltern science" that does not "see", nor does theology itself "examine" its own ultimate foundations. It depends on the "science of the saints", on what they see: their act of seeing is the reference point of theological thinking and the guarantee of its legitimacy.

It follows that the work of the theologian is "secondary" with regard to the real experience of the saints. Without this reference point, without the deep anchoring in such an experience, his work becomes detached from reality. This is the humility demanded of the theologian ... without the realism of the saints, without their contact with the reality of which theology speaks, it degenerates into an empty intellectual game and also loses its scientific character.

2. The verification of faith in life

When we put our confidence in what Jesus sees and believe in his word, we are not in fact moving around in total darkness. The good news of Jesus corresponds to an interior expectation in our heart; it corresponds to an internal light in our being that reaches out to the truth of God. Certainly, we are before all else believers "at second hand". But Saint Thomas is right to describe faith as a process, as an interior path, when he writes: "The light of faith leads us to see." In his Gospel, Saint John draws our attention several times to this process, for example, in the episode of the Samaritan woman who relates what happened to her when she met Jesus and how she recognized in him the Messiah: the Savior discloses to her the path of God and then introduces her to the knowledge of him, which is the source of life. The fact that it is precisely *this* woman who says this compels the people in her village to listen to her words; they believe in Jesus "because of the woman", that is, they believe at second hand. Nevertheless, they invite Jesus to stay with them and so enter into dialogue with him. And at the end they can tell the woman: "It is no longer because of your words that we believe, for we have heard for ourselves, and we know that this is indeed the Savior of the world" (Jn 4:42). In the living encounter, faith is transformed into "knowledge".

It would of course be wrong to imagine the subsequent path of faith as a linear process, as an untrammeled development. Since this path is linked to our life with all its ups and downs, we keep experiencing setbacks that oblige us to start anew. Every phase of life has to discover its own specific maturity, for otherwise we fall back into the corresponding immaturity. And yet, we can say that the life of faith also permits the growth of an evidential character of the faith: its reality touches us, and the experience of a successful life of faith assures us that Jesus is truly the Savior of the world. Here, the second aspect we have just evoked joins the first aspect: in the New Testament, the word "saints" designated Christians as a whole, who certainly did not possess all the qualities that are required in a canonized "saint". But this designation expressed the fact that all were called, in virtue of their experience of the risen Lord, to become a point of reference for others, thus putting them in contact with Jesus' act of seeing the living God. This remains true even today: a believer who allows himself to be formed and guided by the Church's faith, no matter what his weaknesses and difficulties may be, ought to be a window opened onto the light of the living God; and if he genuinely believes, that is what he is. The believer ought to be a force of opposition to the powers that keep the truth a prisoner and to the wall of prejudices that prevents people from seeing God. A faith that is still inchoate ought in some way to find support in him. Just as the Samaritan woman became a living invitation to meet Jesus, so, too, in the darkness of a world that is largely opposed to God, the faith of believers is an essential reference point in the search for God.

3. Faith's "I", "you", and "we"

The mediatory intervention of Jesus and that of the saints (which derives from his) converge in a third reflection. The act of faith is an eminently personal act, anchored in the most intimate depths of the human "I". But precisely by being so personal, it is at the same time an act of communication. In the depths of its nature, the "I" is always linked to the "you", and vice versa: an authentic relationship that becomes "communication" can be born only from the depths of the person. We have said that believing means sharing in what Jesus sees, relying on Jesus; Saint John, who leans on the breast of Jesus at the Last Supper, is a symbol of what faith as such signifies. To believe is to communicate with Jesus, freeing oneself thereby from the repression that is contrary to the truth, freeing my own "I", which is shut up in its own self, and making my "I" a response to the Father: a response to the Yes of love, the Yes pronounced over our existence, that Yes which is our redemption and which overcomes the "world".

In its most intimate nature, faith is therefore a way of "being with" someone, of shattering that isolation of my "I" which is also its malady. The act of faith opens out onto the distant horizon, breaking down the barriers of my subjectivity.

It is this that Paul describes when he says: "It is no longer I who live, but Christ who lives in me" (Gal 2:20).

The "I", dissolved, rediscovers itself in a new and larger "I". Paul describes this process, whereby the first "I" dissolves and wakes up in a larger "I", as a "rebirth". In this new "I", in which liberating faith immerses me, I do not, however, discover that I am united only to Jesus: I am united likewise to all those who have walked along the same path. In other words, faith is necessarily an ecclesial act. It lives and moves in the "we" of the Church, since it makes us one with the "I"-communion of Jesus Christ. In this new subject, the wall separating myself and the others collapses—the wall that separates my subjectivity from the external world and makes it inaccessible to me, the wall between me and the depths of being. In this new subject, I become a contemporary of Jesus, and all the experiences of the Church belong to me. They have become my own experiences.

Naturally, this new birth is not the work of an instant; it lasts throughout the whole course of my life. The essential point here is that I cannot construct my own personal faith in a private dialogue with Jesus. If faith does not live in this "we", it does not live at all. It is impossible to separate faith and life, or truth and life, "I" and "we". It is only within an existence lived in the "we" of believers, in the "we" of the Church, that faith unfolds its own logic and takes on its own organic form.

Let us sum up. As in the questions of everyday, so too in our relationship with God we can find a path forward only by sharing in the knowledge of others. In our relationship with God, those who see and those who experience are present, and we can rely on them in our own faith. In some way, they bestow their own certainty on us. We make up the multitude, but we are not simply blind vis-à-vis God. Relying on those who see, we advance gradually toward him, and the buried memory of God, which is written on the heart of every man, awakens more and more to life in the depths of our own being. When we live close to God, our sight is restored: when we use our eyes, they bear witness to his truth.

Pascal's advice to his friend may seem skeptical, but it is correct: begin with the folly of faith, and you will attain knowledge. This folly is wisdom; this folly is the path of truth.

Cardinal Ratzinger gave this lecture at the School of Catholic Culture, in Santa Croce, in Bassano.